Learning to earn Extra Income by Trading Options

A STEP BY STEP GUIDE

By Timothy Phillips

Learning to Earn Extra Income by Trading Options

Table of Contents

ACKNOWLEGEMENTS

I would first like to take the time to *thank* the LORD, Who is the Head of my life and is the real reason that I have been able to write this book. Thank-You LORD!

Then, I would like to thank my dear sweet mother Janice and each one of my sisters, family members, and friends for their prayers and support which has made it possible for me to write this book.

Introduction

Many people, who make the decision to become retail traders, begin by holding *grand* ideas of becoming wealthy or super rich, simply by starting to trade in the markets with just a few hundred dollars. The truth is this rarely ever happens. It *can* happen, however, but without the right training and experience, it is very, very rare.

Through trial and error and the *loss* of thousands of dollars, some traders finally begin to *see* the error of their ways and actually start using the correct tools (that are readily available to most traders) which allows them to, finally become *profitable* traders. By using these tools effectively, and one in particular that we will learn later, the retail trader can find themselves safely on the road to seriously learning to earn extra income by trading options.

The Aim of This Book

First, let us address in which of the multiple financial markets we are covering in this book. We will be dealing with the US stock market indices, primarily (if not exclusively) the Nasdaq100® index (NDX). More specifically, we will mainly be dealing (step-by-step) with the NDX options market, although what we teach could apply to some other indices and even to some other stocks.

By taking advantage of various trading tools, with one special tool specifically, the retail trader can learn to earn extra income by investing in the NDX index options market. At the same time, having to use only a relatively small amount of investment.

Secondly, we must mention the people to whom this book will benefit most. The individuals who will benefit most from this book are the type of *'Retail Traders'* who have or **will have** (with the goal of saving their money and *learning* to use these basic trading techniques effectively) at least four to six thousand dollars (and thirty thousand, if possible).

Money that will not pose real financial *harm* if lost by trading in the markets. Additionally, this type of trader must have the *time and patience* set aside to learn how to trade the index markets (particularly the NDX market) before risking any investment capital.

Keep in mind, however, the retail trader that follows this program does not necessarily need to have access to tens of thousands of dollars to trade and invest with, in order to be successful. It is much harder, on-the-other-hand, but not impossible, if a trader has only a *few hundred dollars* to begin trading in the markets to become profitable.

The fact remains, however, that I (the author) have put on multiple profitable trades with just a *couple* hundred dollars, yet very few profitable trades in the NDX market with such a small amount of money. Either most of these profitable trades were from stock options (which are more volatile) or from the SPX and RUT indices (which do not move nearly as much as the NDX).

The type of trading we will attempt to explain in this book, however, is *more* affective with a larger account (when compared to a few hundred dollars) of at least a thirty-five hundred dollars or more investment (at this writing). This amount will allow us, as option traders, to invest a somewhat smaller percentage of the account funds in each option trade position, and still remain profitable, compared to having only a few hundred dollars to invest with.

Holding only about a three to ten thousand dollar trading account will *still* give, at the very least, some *cushion* for those who cannot afford any more. At the same time, it will, also, allow traders to enter into a profitable trade position of say around fifteen hundred dollars or so.

The general standard, according to most market trading experts, is to trade one to ten percent of ones' trading account as a whole. Nevertheless, it is possible, (but more risky) to trade half of ones' account with the use of prudent trading practices, and still *preserve* most of the capital in our trading accounts.

Disclaimer:

The stock market and options market are very risky and volatile, and any investor or trader may be subject to lose some or all of their investment capital. Therefore, a person should only use money to invest or trade that will not pose significant financial harm or hardship if lost in the markets.

The author neither of this book, his business, nor the publisher are liable for any losses that may result from the use of any or all of the advice given in this book. It is best to consult a Registered Financial Investment Advisor and Consultant when acting upon the trading advice given in this or any other trading or investment book.

This systematic trading guide does not include many of the conventional trading methods found in most trading books. It does include (necessarily) some conventional techniques and methods that some trading experts have popularized.

These techniques are those that seem to have passed the *test of time* and thus far proven to be very effective in trading. Yet, there are other methods that the reader will discover in this book, that are not as conventional in nature. Therefore, we should test them before putting them to use in real trades.

Subjects Not Covered In depth

At this time, we need to address those subjects that we will not cover, in depth, in this book. The complete understanding of how to use candlestick charts, for instance, although we will cover the subject, it will not be with the type of detail that will make the reader an instant *expert* in candlestick charting.

Having said that, the reader will *not* actually need to be an expert in candlestick charts or any other subject that we will cover in this book, in order to become a profitable trader. This book will attempt to provide enough of the systematic descriptions of the basics that will still properly *equip* the reader to be on the road to learning to earn extra income by trading options.

Furthermore, concerning the other important topics like, for example, how stock options work? This book will cover the subject of options well enough for our purposes of investing, however, it would still be *very* beneficial for the reader to google '*stock options*,' and learn more of what they are, and the multiple strategies involved in trading them. There exists a world of *free* articles, blogs, and social media videos that give *valuable* instructions on trading stocks and options, which are available, at our very fingertips, on the internet.

None-the-less, please be reassured that this book was written with the intention of being *very* informative and educational to everyone from the *beginner* to the *intermediate* Retail Trader. It, also, should be correctly noted that I, the author of this book, am not a *perfect* professional trader to begin with (there is, probably, no such thing as a perfect trader).

I must admit, that I have not mastered, at this writing, all of the various *complex* trading strategies promoted out there by some trading gurus.

In fact, with some of those strategies that I have learned, I have regretfully discovered them to be *total failures* that have cost many traders, including myself, a lot of money in losses by practicing them. No, I am just a *Retail Trader* who has learned from trial and error, having faced the loss of thousands of *real* dollars in some trades, and then the rewarding gain of thousands more of *real* dollars in other trades. In addition, I have been fortunate enough to learn, the hard way, how to properly, view the trading process as a business, while using the right tools to become profitable.

LIST OF WHAT EACH RETAIL TRADER NEEDS

Now, to lay the foundation of what the average retail trader needs to be successful at investing in the NDX options market. There are some 'must-have' items, that each trader needs to acquire (please take notes, if possible):

1. The retail trader needs to open a brokerage account with a *good*, reputable (online) broker, who is set-up for options trading and has low fees, plus has a good virtual trading simulator (very important).
2. He or she MUST, also, have access to a *good* computer, possessing fast (or, at least decent) internet speed that is ready for use on each trading day (which are the normal weekdays that are not Federal Holidays).
3. The retail trader needs to have a good sparrow notebook or journal to use as a daily trading journal.
4. Next, the retail trader needs to have access to some basic online stock market charting websites. These websites should allow him to set up candlestick charts with the moving averages that go with them. He could use any of the free charts that are readily available online. The trader, however, must be careful not to overly depend on

these free charts throughout each trading day because sometimes, free charts tend to lag the actual market trading by as much as fifteen minutes.

5. Then, the trader will need to have the allotted amount of *time,* during normal trading hours, to watch his or her trades.

6. Finally, the retail trader must have access to daily business news. There are multiple free online websites that feature the latest economic, corporate, and stock market news. Keep in mind, however, the business news from most sites might have a delay or lag time in releasing the news to the public.

Now it is time for us to get down to this matter at hand of learning to trade options.

CHAPTER ONE

Honing trading skills

This will possibly be the most important chapter in this book, so please read through it carefully. Once we as market traders understand the need to hone our trading skills before risking any real money, we will be well on our way to having *profitable* trades.

On the other hand, if we as market traders decide that we do not need to learn the markets or learn sound trading strategies before starting to invest our hard-earned money, we will quickly *lose our shirts,* even before we have had enough time to learn the basics of trading.

Please Remember: *It takes time and practice to really, learn to trade consistently and profitably.*

It is interesting to note, that even many *veteran professional* traders sometimes find the need to go back and practice honing their skills, when beginning with a new trading strategy. These professionals do so before they actually put real money behind it. This is one of the things that separates the foolish, and novice traders, from the wise, seasoned and *profitable* traders; practice, and more practice.

Best Way for Traders To Hone Their Trading Skills

Retail traders must use what some believe is one of the best training tools for trading. We must make use of a trading *Simulator* if we are going to hone our trading skills properly.

There is no, 'if,' 'ands,' or 'buts' about it, we as traders *must* practice in a realistic trading platform setting (similar to what we will use to trade real money with) if we are to learn to trade!

The **Trading Simulator** is a virtual or paper-trading platform, which should be *identical* to our broker's *real* online trading platform. This becomes the proving ground for real trading.

As concerning options, the simulator should have the same type of option chains utilized in real trading. The price of the option, as well as the underline stock (that the option is based on) in real time, plus other necessary items, all should be found in the trading simulator platform which we use. The simulator is not a toy, by the way, it is a *tool*; a very **important** tool.

There are some skills needed to properly paper trade (or to virtual trade) with the trading simulator.

How Should Traders Use The Simulator?

There is a right way and a wrong way to use this effective trading tool. The right way for us to use it is to approach it is with the same strategic mentality we would use when trading on a real platform, using real money. That is to say, we should use it as follows:

1. First, we should consider and approach the simulator as a *test* to see if we have what it takes to earn a *real* income from our trading. It is a vital test.
2. Next, we should use the same amount of money in each trading position, which we would actually use when trading with *real* money.
3. Third, we, also, should use the same trading strategies and techniques that we would employ in a real trading

2

situation. This is also a test or proving ground for our strategies, as well as for ourselves.

4. Fourth, we must use a trading journal of some type (a sparrow notebook tablet, or journal) to take notes on each trade that we enter into in the simulator (more on that subject later).

Once we understand the basics of using our particular trading simulator, then we must start to practice, in real time, those methods or strategies that we have learned to use in trading the markets. We must continue to consistently practice, on a daily basis, just as if we were making real trades, on the simulator.

After all that's the purpose of the simulator. Moreover, this is where the rubber meets the road, as the old saying goes. It will be during these times that we should use *all* the knowledge and methodology that we have *learned* about trading, in order to, see what works and what does not work.

Our success or failure will be determined during this period of trading, as well. As we will find with actual real trades, either we will lose money, and see our trading account dwindle, or we will make money and see our trading account (on the simulator) increase with profits.

Whether or not we *consistently* lose our money or gain money, using these trading methods, in either case the trading simulator will actually allow us to view the results for ourselves, up close and personal.

How Long Should A Trader Use the Simulator Trading Platform?

Each trader must decide on their own, or with the help of a *trained financial advisor*, when they are ready to trade on a real trading platform. There is no one right (cookie-cutter) answer for every trader because each person is different. There are some skills, however, that each trader, who wishes to be successful, must find in himself or herself before they are ready to trade with real money.

The best way for a trader to see if they have obtained the necessary skills is to ask themselves some questions that they must answer honestly, *before they are ready.*

First, am I consistently make net gains, after commissions and fees, on my trades overall? The main reason for trading, after all, is *to make money*. When we can clearly see that our trades are *frequently* profitable, than that is a good sign that we have acquired a profitable trading method along with the knowledge to employ it in real time.

Secondly, have I been able to apply my trading methods over various market conditions? It is one thing to make money on *long* trades when there are raging bull markets (or plunging bear markets if we take a *short* position), but it is another thing, altogether, to make profitable trades when the markets are choppy (that is to say, up one minute, and down the next).

We must determine, while using the trading simulator, how our trading ability measures up in most market conditions over an extended period. How long that time will be will depend upon the individual trader.

Next, we will begin to know that we have passed the trading test when we have learned to view trading as though it is a **business**. Despite what most people think, trading is not gambling. Trading can be gambling if the trader does not learn how to, properly *manage risk*. However, if we have the correct mind-set, we will learn to manage each trade as a businessperson would **manage** *multiple* product lines in an uncertain marketplace.

That is to say, we would view pre-market conditions to plan, ahead, only sell what is in-demand, quickly remove products that are not selling, and re-stock products that are strongly selling until the market starts to lose its momentum. This is why we must use a trading journal to track our trades and record market conditions.

Once we have met these three criterion, we are now ready to start trading with real money. Yet, we must never think, however, that we have totally graduated from ever using a trading simulator platform again. There will be times when we will learn the type of new techniques for trading that are not ready for trades involving real money.

The simulator should be a *readily available* friend (from our broker) which we use to practice our new trading ideas before committing any *real* hard-earned money.

Please remember: The purpose of the trading simulator is to save the trader from having *disastrous* financial results.

CHAPTER TWO

How to Trade the Stock Options Market

Why Trade NDX Options?

NDX index options (Nasdaq 100 index®) are good trading vehicles because they usually have extensive price changes. It is nothing to see the NDX index up or down (depending upon the market climate) thirty-five to forty dollars a share. With our method, all we will need, when using an options Delta of thirty, is to have a ten to twenty dollar move in the direction that we are trading in, before we see a decent profit.

Furthermore, with this type of market move, we can be sure to see a profit (at least at this writing) of anywhere from one hundred dollars to five hundred dollars per contract on each day that we are trading.

There are other days when the Nasdaq Composite Index, which is what the NDX index is based upon, has very choppy market conditions. It is up by ten dollars one minute, and down by ten dollars a share the next minute. Among these are the type of market conditions that we need to learn to avoid trading in, and learn to wait until the market fluctuations settles down in one definite market direction.

The Basics of Trading Options

What is an option in the first place? An option is a contract on a stock sold by one individual to another individual, which gives him or her the right, but not the obligation, to either buy or sell the underlying stock at a certain price, and within a particular period, or on a set date. The person buying the option has the right to purchase the stock (if it is a Call option) or to sell the stock (if it is a Put option).

Most of the time, the individual buying the option contract does not intend to actually buy or sell the underlying stock, he usually only seeks to trade the option just to gain a profitable increase in the *option value*, itself. In other words, he is using the option as a trading vehicle in place of the actual underlying stock. Therefore, if he buys an option for one hundred dollars, he intends to sell it, for example, for two hundred dollars, or any amount above what he has purchased it. This means his only desire, really, is to make a *profit* by trading the option contract, itself, on the open market.

Does this sound somewhat familiar?

If the answer is yes, it is because it **is** familiar. It is similar to buying and selling (or, trading) the stock itself. The trader wants to buy low and sell high, and options are not that different. The major difference between the stock option and the underlying stock, is that the stock option is a contract based upon the stock that has an expiration date, while the stock, itself, does not ever really expire, except when (or if) the company is ever dissolved, etc.

In addition, the option (in its most basic form) may be purchased in one of two ways: as shares with the hopes of having the price of usually purchase either a Call or Put option contract, but the stock the shares go up in value. A small percentage of traders actually short sell stocks, hoping that the shares decrease in value, but these are only a small percentage of traders.

The Call option makes money by an *increase* in the underlying stock price, but the Put option only makes money by a *decrease* in the underlying stock price. In either case, the option will *increase* in value when the underlying stock price trends in direction that the trader has entered a position in (whether it is a long position or a short position).

Let us just say that, for example, the trader buys a **Call option** on ABC Co. stock for five hundred dollars, holding hopes that the stock price will rise in value. The underlying stock price is now at fifty dollars a share when the trader first buys the Call option contract. Later, the underlying stock price, then, increases to fifty-five dollars a share. This now means that the Call option will increase in value to six hundred dollars per contract (for example).

Now, the trader happily has earned a one hundred dollar profit (minus commissions and fees, of course) if he sells or exits the call option contract. On the other hand, if the stock decreases in price to, say, forty-five dollars a share, in this case the call option will also decreases in value.

This time, it becomes worth only four hundred dollars per contract. Therefore, if the trader sells the Call option contract, in this instance, he will have to face a one hundred dollar *loss,* with commission and fees that only add to the loss.

There are actually many other factors that affect the option's value, however, (like, strike price, Delta, implied volatility, Theta, gamma, etc.) that the trader should learn more about before starting to trade. We, however, will touch on those later, but for now, we are trying to use the most *simplistic* manner to describe how basic options works.

Now, let us focus on how a **Put option** works in its most basic form. Again, we want the Put option contract to increase in value, in order to make a profit, in the same way that we wanted the Call option to increase in value to make a profit. The difference here is that the Put option is like a short (or sell) of the stock, which means that the Put option only makes money when the underlying stock price *decreases* or lowers in value.

Using ABC Co. stock again, let us say the trader bought a Put option contract on ABC Co. stock, with hopes that the stock price goes down. He buys it for five hundred dollars per contract while the underlying stock price of ABC Co. is at fifty dollars a share. Now, let us say the price drops to forty-five dollars a share, and then the Put option will now be worth six hundred dollars per contract, because the Put option only gains value when the underlying stock decreases in value.

Hence, it is like shorting the stock and only profiting when the stock drops in price per share. Therefore, a Call option wants stock up in value and a Put option wants stock down in value. It is that simple.

With the basic understanding of what a Call option and a Put option are, we now should see that the price change of the underlying stock or index is *very* important. Therefore, if we (as traders) are to know when to buy an option contract based on the (underlying) stock, we need a certain methodology to be able to tell us when the stock is going up (for a Call option contract) or down (for a Put option contract).

This is where candlestick stock charts and other indicators become necessary tools, because they actually can enable a trader to predict, with high or low probability, the direction of the stock price movement. But more on charts and indicators later, for now, however, we are going to focus on the basic process of buying ABC Co. stock options from our online broker.

Understanding Option Chains

Once we have decided to buy ABC Co. stock options, we must login to our online brokerage account and proceed to the option chains that represent ABC Co. stock options. Depending on the broker, options page will show two long sections of price levels (or chains), one for Put options (usually on the right side) and one for the Call options (usually located on the left side).

Then, there is a section that is (many times, but not always) located down the middle, which is generally comprised of all of the Strike Prices, for both the Call and the Put option chains.

The **Strike Price** is the price that the trader predicts the underlying stock price will become at some point in the near future, before the option contract expires. It is like saying, 'This stock or index is heading to this particular price sometime in the near future.' Moreover, if we are right, then we will probably make a profit, but if we are wrong, we will probably lose money once we exit the trade. Therefore, whenever we buy a Call or a Put option contract, we must buy it at the strike price that represents what we *predict* (or believe) the underlying stock will be at in the near future.

The Call and the Put sections in the options chain each have a highlighted area known as the **In-The-Money** area, which is in the upper half of the Call options section and in the lower half of the Put option section. Being in the money simply means (in the case of the Put) that the strike prices are higher in value than the current market price of the underlying stock, and (in the case of the Call) the strike price is *lower* in price value to the current market price.

Without going into much detail, the option chain also gives us the choice of expiration dates that we might want to buy for an option. These dates could range anywhere from one week expiration, to a one year expiration. Be aware, however, that the further out an option contract will expire, the higher the price of that option.

It is, also, important to note that the price of the option at each strike price represents only **one share** of stock. Yet, each option contract is composed of one hundred shares. Therefore, we must multiply that price shown on the option chain by one hundred before we will get the *real* cost we must pay before commissions and fees.

Usually the commissions and fees together are less than fifteen dollars, depending on the online broker that each trader is using. Some brokers have much lower fees than that (like three or four dollars), while others have somewhat higher fees, but most are less than fifteen dollars per trade.

We, also, must realize that we are charged fees each time we enter *and* each time we exit a trade position. Therefore, we are charged commissions and fee, first, to enter the trade, and then **again,** whenever we exit the option trade. Keep this in mind.

Another cost that the trader needs to be aware of is the cost of the Option *Spread.* The Spread is the difference in price between the Bid and the Ask. The *Ask* is the set price that we *must* pay in order to purchase the option. Whereas, the *Bid* is the set price that we *must* sell the option for, in order to exit the position.

The difference in price is a *built-in fee* that goes to the floor traders or market makers (or their companies) who execute the trades on our behalf. The Spread can be negotiable, but usually only for those traders with very large accounts or with many daily trades. Yet, for all other traders, however, it is *non-negotiable,* for the most part depending on the broker. In addition, we have to be pay it before we can buy an option contract.

We also, must take into consideration, in our trading plans, the *cost* of the Spread. On some stock options, it might be just a few dollars, on others; however, it could be as high as three hundred or more dollars. Keep in mind, that this is a built-in loss, which we must face. Which translates to mean, as far as our trading strategy is concerned, that the option we invest in, must increase in price value enough to cover the losses from our trading commissions and fees, and the losses from the Spread to order to break even.

Any trading strategy, plan, or method that is used, should take into account each of these built-in losses from the Spread and the commissions with all fees. The commissions and fees, however, are usually *much less* than the cost of the Spread, and normally have a smaller effect on profits or losses than that of the Spread.

What else can we find in the option chains?

The Greeks are other important items found in option chains. The **Greeks** are a set of Greek alphabet terms (all except implied volatility) used to represent the *risks* involved at each option chain level, for any given strike price (strike price being the predicted price level of the underlying stock before the chosen expiration date).

They represent how the option price is influenced by certain changes in the underlying stock price. Basically, they let us know that just because an underlying stock moves up one dollar in value, does not necessarily mean that the option on that stock will move up exactly one dollar in value, it all just depends on the Greeks for each option.

There are six Greeks that are important to the stock option value or price, but only four that really are important for us. There is the Delta, Theta, Vega, and Implied Volatility. Each one tells us how the option price (or value) will be changed when a stock moves up or down by one dollar. The **Delta**, for instance, tells us *how much*, in percentage of a dollar, the option price will increase or decrease with each dollar change in the underlying stock. Once we multiply this number by one hundred, than we will have the added dollar amount that is to the price of the option with each increase or decrease of one dollar in the underlying stock.

Having said that, we should note that a good Delta, which I (the author) uses, is around 30. This Delta number is *not set in stone,* and each options trader must decide for himself or herself, which Delta is most profitable for the money they are willing to invest.

Next, there is the Greek call **Theta**. Theta is just the amount, multiplied by 100, as always, that the option price will lose in value each trading day, as it gets closer to expiration. At expiration, the option loses *all* value and literally becomes *worth nothing*. That is why it is important to trade (or cash-in) the option before the expiration date.

Next, we have **Implied Volatility**. This is a very important Non-Greek factor for most option traders to know. Although implied volatility is not an actual Greek, it is usually *included* among the other Greeks. Implied Volatility is the rate of price fluctuations in the underlying stock. Higher implied volatility usually increases the premium on the option.

In some the cases, high implied volatility causes the option is to be overpriced. This can be a good thing for the options trader who owns the option while the implied volatility is steady rising, because the price of the option will start multiplying in value. It also, can be a negative thing if the volatility is decreasing while the options trader owns the option contract because this time, the price of the option might be decreasing in value leading to a loss.

Beside implied volatility, there are other measures of volatility like the Historical volatility (or the volatility exactly one year ago), and the Statistical Volatility (which is the volatility as it relates to time and price). For our purposes with options, however, implied volatility is the key factor to understand.

Finally, you have the Greek called *Vega*. Vega is the influence that the volatility of the underlying stock has on the price value of the option. This means for every 1% change in volatility of the stock, the price of the option will increase or decrease by whatever the Vega amount is.

Gamma is another Greek that is not as important for trading the NDX, yet the options trader still needs to know. Gamma is the rate of change in the delta for every one-dollar change in the price of the underlying stock. The higher the Gamma, the quicker you will see the Delta respond (either higher or lower in value) to changes in the underlying stock price. Which translates to a higher probability of better profits.

Keep these Greeks in perspective when you are choosing to buy options from your option chains. They could make the difference as to whether it is wise to invest in certain option strike prices versus other strike prices.

Alternatively, they will inform us as to whether we should be trading options that particular day or not. Remember, at times it is *more* profitable to *Stay Out* of the market than to get in. Never rush to get into a trade without doing *all due diligence* to ensure that we will make a profit and be able to exit the market in a relatively *short* period.

Choosing the Best Expiration Date

All stock and index options have an expiration date. The option generally expires on the third Saturday after the third Friday of each month. In other words, the option *really,* for all practical purposes, expires the third Friday of the month in a one-month option; this is the **standard expiration** period for all options.

One can choose, however, to buy options with expirations that are several months in advance. One can even buy an option that expires a year in advance. In addition, whether we believe it or not, we can even buy weekly options if we so choose to do so.

Note: We should be very careful when buying options that are *in the money,* not to let them expire, if we do not have no intend to purchase the underlying stock. The reason for this is that our broker, usually, automatically charges our account for the underlying stock at the strike price that we chose. Therefore, always sell *In-The-Money* options before they expire or we will *automatically purchase* the underlying stock regardless of whether we want it or not.

The Best expiration date that I, the author, uses when trading NDX options is the *standard* monthly options. I like these options when they are set to expire anywhere from two weeks to forty-five days (which is the next standard option month). Sometimes, I even use weekly options that have two or more weeks to expire. Again, this is my opinion based on my personal trading experiences, and it is not set in stone.

We can use other strategies for weekly options and for options that have expirations that are sixty, ninety days, and even a year in advance. Nevertheless, for this writing, two weeks to forty-five days using mainly *standard* expiration dates, creates the ideal trading atmosphere for earning a good return on investment.

Consequently, we must be very careful, when we are about to enter a position, to ensure that what is displayed in the purchase box is our chosen expiration date and not the one that the platform chooses by *default*. An options trader can get in *real* trouble when she or he jumps into a position quickly without checking and reviewing their order first.

Therefore, it is necessary to trade with an online broker who has a good *trading simulator* because it allows the options trader to practice and become familiar with that particular platform, before risking *real* money.

CHAPTER THREE

Profitable Trading Methods

Once we have become familiar with the trading platform and the options chains by virtual or paper trading with a trading simulator, it will become necessary for us to put the profitable trading practices to the test on these platforms. We are now ready to discover the best trading methods and strategies leading to the most *optimal* trading results.

When it comes to trading the NDX options, Momentum and Breakout trading methods are best in my (the author's) Retail trading experience. On a personal note, I have found that momentum trading mixed in with a little breakout trading is the safest and most profitable method that any options trader can use in order to trade with limited risk. These methods focus on the underlying stock or index's price movement and volatility.

In **Momentum** trading, for instance, the trader is only trading when there is a large and consistent move (jump, leap, or plunge) in the stock (or, in this case, the index) that is, also, in keeping with the trend. A **trend** is the general direction, over a certain period time, that the stock is moving along. The trend can be up, down, or even sideways.

When there is strong breakout and consistent movement in the price of the stock or index, usually in the direction of the trend, then this may be a good set-up to begin trading in, provided it have all the other necessary factors in tack.

As concerning the trend, most professional traders believe that it is *hard* to trade *successfully* against the trend. Another thing to understand is that the trend can be as short as a five, fifteen,

17

thirty-minute trend, or even an hourly trend. Alternatively, it could be as long as a daily, weekly, and even three-month (long) trend.

Whatever the period, the options trader should only buy options that are in the direction of the *momentum-moving* trend of the underlying stock or index.

A better way to describe trading with market momentum is to think of a volatile market as the rocky, whitewater rapids of a riverbed, which flows with great turbulence. Moreover, think of each trader as individuals in a raft trying to maneuver their raft across the rocky riverbed. If they try to maneuver their rafts against the tide and current flow direction of the rapids, they will quickly find themselves at risk of being either *overturned* or *bashed* against a large rock in a sudden tidal wave shift. They could easily lose their raft to the mighty rapids and find themselves in deep trouble.

Considering this same scenario, if the traders point their rafts in the direction of the flow of the current, the river will quickly, and somewhat safely, carry them, with little effort on their part, toward their destination. At the same time, the rapids might become too turbulent and choppy to *risk getting in* the river.

During these times, it is safer to stay out of the river and on the sidelines than to try to risk the possibility of overturning in turbulent waters. The moral of this illustration is to teach us the *dangers* of trading against a very *momentous* trend. Although there will be curves and short shifts in the direction of the current, if we row our rafts *in the general direction* of the current flow, our journey will become a profitable one.

What is breakout trading?

Breakout trading is simply trading only when a stock price has broken through *above* or *beneath* the support or resistance lines on a stock chart, to become either a strong upward trend or downward trend. The price has broken out of the box, if you will, from the price movement trap that it was in for a certain period.

While the price was in this invisible box, it went up the hill in value and then down the hill, and back up and then down the hill again, in a somewhat orderly succession. It stayed within a certain price range called: the ***Price Channel***. On the price chart, the price channel is evident because it rather reminds one of a *sine* wave over a particular period.

The breakout comes when the price leaves the top invisible borderline of the sine wave (also known as the ***Resistance*** line) or it leaves the bottom invisible borderline of the sine wave (commonly known as the ***Support*** line).

As long as the breakout candle (on a candlestick price chart) has a slightly *larger body* than any other candle in the price channel, plus the breakout candle has *not surged too far above* the price channel, then a new trend is beginning to take shape. Our trading can benefit from some breakout trades.

Also, understand that in order for an option to increase in value and become profitable, their **needs to be a certain amount of volatility in the market**. If the market is having a directional trend, but is moving like a *turtle*, there may not exist enough volatility in the market to have it defined as a *breakout trade*. There has to be some surge in price before we can be positive that we have a breakout trade.

Furthermore, it is a good idea to have a mental support (or, baseline price) and a mental resistance (or, ceiling price) in our minds as we are watching the *price alone*. Many times, we will find that just by watching the price by itself, we can see a *surge* of momentum in the price. If we see that the price has been in a sustained direction and has some breakout in price, we should plan to enter or exit the market once we see that the price has passed a certain price point.

The day trading option

Day trading, though risky, can be a way, along with swing trading, to trade stock options in a manner similar to how one would *day trade* stocks. What is day trading? **Day trading**, to begin with, is when a trader enters a trade position one day and exits that position on the same day. In order for most brokerage firms to identify an account as being a pattern day trading account, the account must have, at least twenty-five thousand dollars *minimum* (including the amount of money already invested in any open trade positions).

If the account has less than twenty-five thousand dollars, it will not have the same day trading status and is, therefore, limited for trades per week or per rolling five trading day period that it can have.

Most accounts that do not meet the standard minimum set account size, are *still* allowed to have usually three day trades per week or per rolling five trading day period (the period begins with the first day trade). This means that we can take advantage of these three days to enter and exit our trades on the same day, and thereby *limiting* our risk of losing money like someone with a much larger account.

Why? The longer traders hold a position, the higher their probability of having the market change directions on them (especially the Dow or the NASDAQ) overnight, causing them to lose money. Therefore, when traders can enter a trade position during a profitable market climate, and then exit that position after realizing a profit, on the same day, they have now *limited* their risk.

The purpose of this trading method is to limit risk by utilizing each allowed day trade to secure profits before the market changes directions.

As we are learning to earn extra income by trading options, we should discover that we could earn more by using our allotted day trades than by using swing trades. ***Swing trading,*** is when a trader holds a trade position for more than one trading day. Each trader, regardless of their account size, can only have as many swing trades as possible.

In some instances, swing trading may even be warranted, especially when the market indicators and market sentiment suggests a strong, prolonged, market trend in one direction. At this point, if our trade is not yet profitable, it might be prudent to leave this position open for more than one trading day.

Yet, this is still risky; because market climates tend to, sometimes, change overnight. Which means, basically, if we are in an open position when the market starts trending against us in the opposite direction, (especially while we are holding option contracts) than we might actually lose more than half of our money; and that is not a good thing. Therefore, holding a position longer than one day might be *more* risky than closing-out our options positions early, and losing only a small amount of our money.

It might just mean the difference between losing a few hundred dollars and wasting one good day trade, or losing fifteen hundred dollars (if we do not use a stop-loss) just to keep that day trade intact.

Therefore, which would we prefer most, losing a few hundred dollars and exiting a bad trade, or keeping the bad trade position open and losing half or more of the value of our option? This is where the business mind-set comes into play; it allows us to *weigh our options* based on the amount risk involved.

IMPORTANT NOTE: Brokerage firms do **NOT** traders allow to Day Trade with unsettled funds. This means, if a trader has a four thousand dollar account, once he completed a day trade for say, three thousand dollars, and made a profit of three hundred dollars, he will still not allowed to day trade with any of the thirty-three hundred dollars until the next trading day when the funds have *settled*. This would leave him with only one thousand dollars available to day trade.

Most brokerage firms, however, **do** allow the use of all of the funds (including the unsettled thirty-three hundred dollars) in our account, to enter a trade that we will stay in overnight or longer.

On the next trading day, however, *all* of the funds in our account will be considered settled funds (in the case of options) allowing us to day trade again. In the case of day trading *stocks*, themselves, it is different because it takes three trading days to settle funds on stock trades for most brokers. Options, in this regard, are better.

Using a trading Journal

It is very important for those of us who are retail traders to use a trading journal to record both our trades and the market climate that we are trading in. A ***Trading Journal*** is just a notebook (the original type of notebook by the way) where all of the relevant market information is documented, having to do with each trade or potential trade. It gives us the advantage of having our own written record of how the market behaves based on various economic crisis and conditions. Furthermore, it leaves us with a tangible record of our accomplishments in our trading.

It is a good idea to write down the most pertinent information about our trades. We want to be sure to periodically note the time, the price change, and the value of the Dow (including any negative or positive sign symbols that appear which suggest the market direction) while we are holding a position in the market. This will allow us to study any good or bad points that we have found in the market and in our trades.

It is also, a good idea to take notes on what we have discovered while learning to earn extra income by trading options. We should mark down any new discovery about the market that we have not yet previously known. Including this type of information in our trading journals can only serve to better equip us for trading more profitably.

When to Stay Out of the Market

Let us face it some traders always want to be *in* the market in order to feel secure that they are not missing out on profits, while others would rather be *out* of the market to feel secure that their previously earned profits have been safeguarded. None-the-less, whenever we see the Dow and the NASDAQ fluctuating up and then down in price, without a consistent directional move or trend, then we should consider that the market is holding up a big sign that says, **'Keep Out!'**

When the market is fluctuating and uncertain, it is not the time to *risk* any of our hard-earned money. A choppy market is a *Dangerous* market for profits. During this type of market, our business instincts should take over and cause us to realize that it is more profitable to stay *out* of the market, until we see a sustained trend, than to get into the market and possibly lose a lot of money in a very short period.

Furthermore, a choppy market can be a *very tricky* market. In that, it might *appear* to have developed a trend in one particular direction, in just a short amount of time, only to then, turn and begin another short trend in the exact opposite direction.

This happens often in uncertain markets. We must wait and let a sustained trend develop in the market that is in harmony with market price *indicators*, the economic *news* climate of the day, and market *momentum.*

The clue that a market has *fake momentum* is when you see maybe only a few minor jumps in a certain direction, and then slow, very slow movement (like a turtle) toward that direction. *It is as if the market is having second thoughts and it is pausing to think about where it really wants to go.* Whereas, the clue to *real* market momentum is when we see multiple jumps, even leaps, or plunges in a single sustained market trend. Then, the next thing we see is some minor pullbacks, followed by another jump or plunge (depending on the direction of the market) along the same path.

NOTE: Choppy and uncertain markets have a bad tendency to *eat up both the profits and the entire accounts* of many retail and *professional* traders, so really **beware**!

There are, also, other times when it is wise to stay out of the market as well. On the day before Federal holidays, for instance, trading is usually weak and sometimes inconsistent in the markets as many traders are away on vacation while others are exiting positions in order to sustain their accounts during the holiday season.

The hours leading up to important Federal Reserve (the FED) press releases, is another time when it is wise to *stay out* of the market, due to the uncertainty, until they are finished releasing of all of the information. Then, the hours before the Federal government releases periodic economic data on the national economy (like the GDP report for example), we can see a somewhat choppy market climate. Therefore, we must be careful before entering the market during any of these periods.

CHAPTER FOUR

Understanding the Candlestick Price Chart

Defining Price Action with Candlesticks

Probably the most important element of our trading method is price action. **Price Action** is the movement of the price of each share of stock or index fund throughout a particular trading period. It is, established by market sentiment where there is an epic battle for control of the price by the bulls (who represent buyers) and the bears (who represent the sellers).

On some days, the bulls are in control and the market reaches higher price levels. On other days, the sellers are in control and the market plummets to lower prices. In either case, we need a system which properly expresses the market sentiment for that day (or whichever period) so that we can see a pattern of where the market is heading.

Before we can properly combine our trading methods and practices into one cohesive trading strategy, it is important that we have a basic understanding of the Price Chart. The price chart is, for all practical purposes, a *visible depiction* of all of the price action that is in the market during a particular trading period.

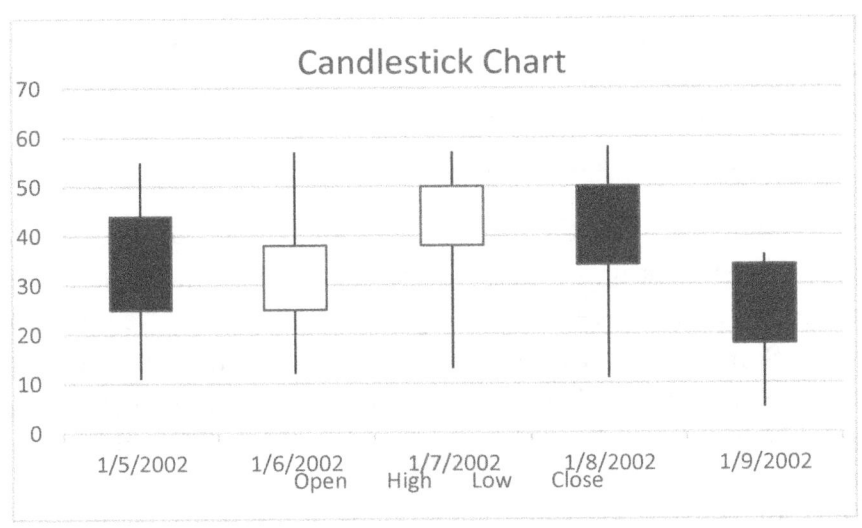

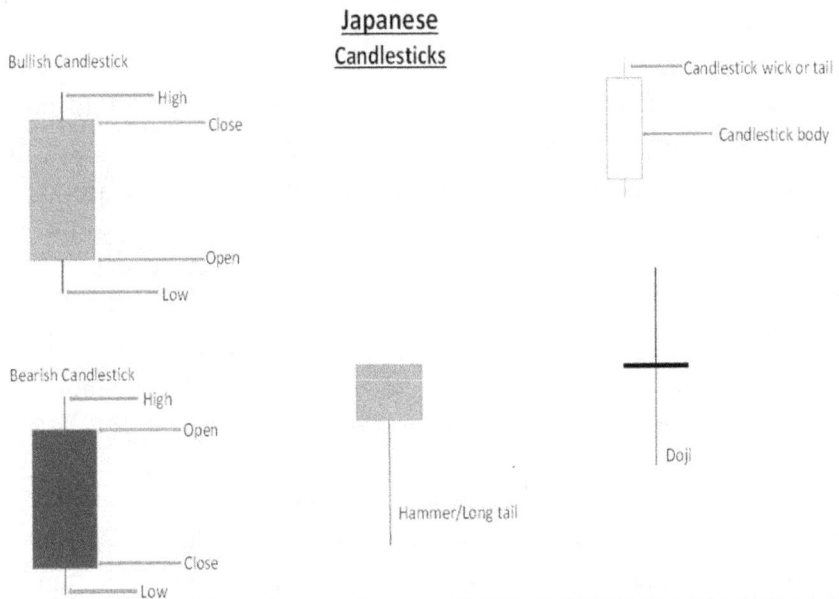

The previous illustration shows a group of Japanese Candlesticks that represent just a few of the multiple shapes and sizes that these candlesticks are found in, when representing general market sentiment. One of the more active candlesticks that is located in most candlestick charts is the **Doji** (shown in the illustration).

Whenever you see, a doji there is a good possibility of a market reversal, especially when there is a large gap between the previous candlestick and the doji. If not, then the doji simply represents a *continuation* of that market trend.

The important thing for our purposes is to look for a *long tail* (also called wick or a shadow) candlestick. One where the tail is at least two or three times longer than the actual candlestick body. Some well-known market traders have stated that any long tailed candlestick pointed in the direction of the trend (that is, either above the 20 EMA or below it) is a signal candlestick.

Once we see the next candlesticks close below that long tail (if it is in the downward trend), or close above that long tail (if it is in an upward trend) than the trend is going to continue.

On the other hand, another school of thought suggests that most long tailed candlesticks signal a reversal in trend. The longer the tail to body ratio the greater the chance that a reversal of trends in the opposite direction that the tail is pointing toward is coming.

I (the author) have seen it both ways, but primarily, I have seen when the tail or wick is more than twice the length of the body of the candlestick, there will be a reversal against whichever direction that the tail is pointing.

The reason for this is that long tailed candlesticks represent a strong push by bullish traders, when the body is located near the top of the candlestick. On the other hand, the long tailed candlesticks represent a strong *selling spree* by the bearish traders in the market, when the body of the candle is located near the bottom of the candlestick.

Therefore, when we see a long tail pointed up on the upward trend, if the next candlestick closes above the tail, it is a continuation of that trend. On the contrary, if we see a long tail that is pointing up in an upward trend, if the next candlestick closes below that candle than it is in a reversal pattern.

INDICATORS

Market traders fall into one of two categories: either they are Fundamental traders (who trade solely based on corporate earnings, revenues, management, and market share), or they are Technicians (who trade solely based upon price action, price charts and indicators). The majority of short-term market traders are technicians who rely almost entirely on price action, price charts, and technical indicators.

There are varieties of market indicators that are in use in today's markets. Indicators, or rather **Technical Indicators**, are simply trading tools used to explain and define the market direction of various financial market places. Some are composed of complex ratios, while others are just simple averages.

The main indicators that we, as options traders, should concern ourselves with are the moving averages indicators. These indicators appear as horizontal lines located across the price charts. Specifically, the 20 EMA, which is the 20 Exponential Moving Average, is very important to us. Additionally, the 50 SMA, or Simple Moving Average, and the 8 EMA each help define the past and forecast the future direction of the price action.

The **20 EMA** represents the most recent price action and, usually, defines the latest trend of the markets. In fact, it has been said that the line of the 20 EMA actually *slopes and points* in the direction of the latest trend. When it slopes up, the trend is up and when it slopes down the trend is, then, down.

Moreover, the 20 EMA provides for us a line that separates the upward market from the downward market. This means that if the

29

prices are above the 20 EMA line, then the price action is in an upward trend. Whereas, if the prices fall below the 20 EMA line on the chart, then the price action is in a downtrend. Thus, the 20 EMA is one of the most important indicators that we will use.

Besides the 20 EMA, we have the 50 SMA or 50 simple moving average. It gives us a much larger outlook of a particular market. It will tell us how the market is trending based upon a longer period. If the price falls below the *50 SMA* line, it is in a longer-term downtrend, and, conversely, if the price rises above the 50 SMA, it is in a longer-term uptrend.

Furthermore, some experts teach that you should only buy (or, use Calls) when the price is above the 50 SMA and you should only sell (or, use Puts) when the price is below the 50 SMA. Personally, I look at price action, and sometimes you will find that the upward trend begins even while the price is still below the 50 SMA. This is just from personal observations, and each trader should determine the right market points to enter and exit for himself or herself.

The 8 EMA (Exponential Moving Average) is used by some experts in a shorter span of time, the same way that the 50 SMA is used in a longer period of time. The *8EMA* represents the latest Buy/Sell line over a short period. Again, this may be subjective, and traders must determine for themselves if this fits the trading set-ups that they are using.

VOLUME

Although the NASDAQ usually does not show any of the trading volume for the NDX index, volume is still very important in our trading, and we should still mention it in this writing. *Volume* is an indicator, in and of itself, which represents the amount of trades processed in each market. Spikes in volume usually accompanies large movements in the price action of stock or other financial market vehicles.

Vertical rectangular bars located below the price charts usually represent volume. One other tool that works well with our volume indicator is the daily average line that runs across the volume bars showing where each volume bar is as it relates to the average daily volume.

Once we see a volume bar surging high above the average daily volume line with a corresponding high price bar on the price chart, then we should realize that large market movers and shakers have entered this particular market (be it a stock, an index, or even currency market).

In addition, we can be sure that the price of that market will move in the direction of the major buying or selling represented by that large volume. We also, must be aware that the price may usually *reverse*, on first the day or two after that big volume move. Yet we be sure that the price will shortly move *solidly* in the direction of that particular volume spike. Again, most of the major indices do not show average daily volume; therefore, we should use the price action with other indicators instead.

CHAPTER FIVE

The sources behind most market moves

SMART MONEY

Probably for over one hundred years individuals collectively known as *smart money,* have controlled the value and the combined point movements of all of the major stock and financial markets all around the world. Many retail investors and retail traders foolishly believe that they can affect the price of stocks and currency markets with their tens of thousands of dollars in investments.

This cannot be any farther from the truth. Thousands, hundreds of thousands, or even a few millions of dollars, in general, cannot move stocks, currencies, and future markets.

Literally, it takes tens of millions, hundreds of millions, and even billions of dollars in trades to move the price and direction of the major markets. Now maybe, if we are referring to *penny stocks*, where the value of the stocks might be as low as ten cents a share, then those markets are open to manipulation by tens of thousands of dollars.

Yet, those markets are *extremely risky and unpredictable* due to the massive manipulation of these stocks. Therefore, conventional wisdom does not recommend purchasing these type of stocks. None-the-less, we must remember, takes the buying power of smart money to actually determine the value and price of stocks, bonds, currency, and future markets.

The question that many ask is whom exactly are these powerful investors and traders commonly referred to as Smart Money?

32

Smart Money is just another name used to describe the big money investors representing large hedge funds, mutual funds, large investment banks, major retirement funds, and extremely wealthy individual investors across the globe. These large firms (and there are hundreds, if not thousands of them) combined literally invest *trillions of dollars* in the financial markets on a daily basis.

Their enormous capital reserves enables them to have the type of organizational infrastructures which gives them the ability to collect and utilize the most valuable information and reports from the markets, even before they start to trickle down to the average retail trader and investor. They can use their *massive* buying power to legally corner and move the markets in ways that benefit them, and takes away the capital of the average retail traders, at the same time. Hence, that is why they are, sometimes called *smart money.*

Compared to them, the average investor that trades with only a few thousand dollars does not even register on the financial Richter scale. Combined, however, hundreds of thousands of these minor investors and traders together represent hundreds of millions, if not billions of dollars in the markets on a daily basis.

For this reason, smart money sees these, mostly retail and financially uneducated investors, as a source of profits ripe for the taking. That is why trying to trade against the trend of the markets is like a go-cart trying to face down a huge train; it is ran over and quickly *wiped out.*

The best way to deal with smart money is to invest *with* them and *not against* them. That is to say, to get in after them and get out before them. Whenever we are about to put on a trade, it is not always easy to tell when exactly smart money has entered our particular market. One of the major clues used by many traders to tell when smart money has entered a stock, for example, is when the volume spikes high above the average daily volume amount.

However, as stated before, the NDX index does not show us volume for the NASDAQ.

There are other telltale signs, which we, as NDX options traders, can use to determine approximately, when smart money has entered the market. One notable sign, which alert us that smart money has entered a particular market, is when we see a *major spike* in the index price.

Since we now know that only smart money-type investment can move the price of markets, this can be a good signal for us. Regardless, there will still the need for us to look for other directional momentum shifts in the market besides price (which will be described later), before it is safe for us to enter the market.

The Harmony of Major Indexes

The Dow Jones Industrial Average, the NASDAQ Composite Index, and S&P 500 index are the chief indexes (or indices) used in the U.S. and around the world to represent the overall stock market sentiment, condition, and performance. Each are composed of multiple companies representing a variety of mostly American and some foreign corporate industries and sectors. Many experts believe that as these major indexes go, so goes the stock and financial markets around the world.

Generally, they move in harmony with one another. Whenever the Dow is down, usually the NASDAQ and the S&P 500 are also down, and conversely, whenever the Dow is up, so the NASDAQ and the S&P 500 seem to follow suit. This is their normal pattern of movement, but there are times when the NASDAQ might be up but the Dow is down, and this mostly only occurs when Tech companies' stocks are under heavy trading, particularly during Earnings season.

During **Earnings Season**, which occur on a quarterly basis, all publicly traded companies must publicly report their earnings and revenues over the past quarter, and they must *forecast* future earnings for the next three or four quarters. In addition, at this time, high tech companies, and others that make-up the NASDAQ, report earnings that can cause significant *spikes* in the NASDAQ, which might, sometimes, break away firmly in the opposite direction from the Dow.

Therefore, we should pay *close attention* to the earnings reports released by the major tech companies during these periods. By doing so, it allows us to gage the market by seeing when any of these companies' stock suddenly jumps, pulls back, or plunges in value. Usually, the financial news media will alert the public on any such massive moves in stocks throughout these seasons.

When we see a stock suddenly rising five or six percent (representing a rise by thirty or forty dollars a share) in value during this period, then we must take note on how the NASDAQ responds to this and other major stock movements. When the earnings reports and forecasts are good for several major companies all at once, and we see the rising significantly in NASDAQ value, then it might well be a good trade opportunity for us, as along as the Dow and S&P are either moving in sync, or have not moved too much in the opposite direction.

On the other hand, if we see all of the markets for instance, moving in a downward direction, yet we see a major NASDAQ company rising by (for example) sixty dollars a share, then this is will not be the best time to trade NDX options because this one stock may affect the entire market.

Trading opportunities for us are greater when the major market indexes are in harmony with one another.

JUMPS, PLUNGES, AND LEAPS

The point value of the Dow Jones Industrial Average, which is the major primary market indicator, along with Nasdaq, and S&P 500, will never move exactly in a straight lined, instead it oscillates and fluctuates up and down (it hops up, *and pulls back,* if you will) throughout the trading day. If the Dow *plunges* more than ten to twelve points within minutes or seconds, and then continues to *slowly* move downward over a longer time frame, than the Dow maybe heading in a downward trend direction.

On the other hand, if the Dow *jumps* up ten to twelve points, and slowly continues to move up, than it is probably heading in an upward direction. How long it will be heading in this direction is uncertain, it could be anywhere from one minute to four days. It all depends upon the market climate, and on the present national economic sentiment held by the smart money investors.

If, at some point, the market turns downward, as a result of some bad economic forecasts coming from either some FED or the Federal government reports, than there is a good chance that the Dow will stay in a downward direction, at least, for the rest of that trading day.

Conversely, if the market suddenly jumps higher, and begins to slowly move (throughout the trading day) in an upward direction, as result of some positive FED and Federal government news, than it has a good chance of staying high, at least for the remainder of that trading day.

All market movements that are coordinated with the national economic news of the day coming from the federal government or the FED, are usually momentum type of movements. The

36

market as we know now, in general, moves like a roller coaster. It moves slightly up, then pulls back a little ways down, then, it moves upward, then really pulls back toward a downward direction, just as a matter of course. At times in the market, there might be little hops, major leaps, or even sudden *plunges* a particular trend direction.

The most important question we must consider for our strategy is, in *which* direction is the market now heading toward, after the *sudden spikes, leaps, or plunges* in price values.

These sudden large movements in price value tend to hit investor's stop-losses hard, causing many traders to have their trades stopped-out. One jump or plunge by three or four points in the opposite direction may not be as serious as, say, having *multiple* jumps/plunges in the exact opposite direction of our position. It is at this point, when we must decide whether to cut our losses and get out of the positions altogether that we are trading in.

Whereas the leaps, on the other hand, usually are a positive sign that the market is trending in one sure direction. Yet, we should still verify, by considering all other factors related to sound momentum movements.

Using Stop Losses for Trades

There comes a time with every options trader where we have to make a decision whether to get out of a trade early, even before our stop losses have hit, or stay in the trade facing a significant risk. It could mean the difference between gaining a *quick* profit, and having to suffer a *great* loss.

While we are learning to earn extra income by trading options, we will discover that stop losses can be very valuable in that they help us to maintain the earnings that we have already

37

accumulated. On the other hand, they can be instrumental in preventing us from making a substantial profit.

In order to prevent this from becoming an issue, it is a good idea to take the time to *monitor* our trade positions with the surrounding markets, throughout the trading day. We need to keep an eye on our trades to allow us to see both: (a) when the markets have suddenly pulled *away* from our position; or (b) when the markets have sharply moved *toward* our position.

By keeping a close eye on our trades, it allows us to make the necessary quick decisions concerning our trades at the best time for us. Thereby, enabling us to either take a quick profit on our trades, or take a smaller loss before our stop loss have triggered. It really does take time to be able to trade profitably.

Speaking of Stop losses, what are they anyway?

A **Stop Loss** is a *preset* amount of loss that the investor sets in a trade that takes them *automatically* out of the trade. Stop Losses can be set in percentage points or in actual dollar amounts. Many trading educators *demand* that their students use stop losses to prevent the sudden loss of the entire amount that they invested in each trade position. They usually teach that having stop losses in place will override the emotions that often get in the way of profitable trading.

One thing that I (the author) have found, however, is that sometimes-tight stop losses (such as those set at ten to twenty percent) are not feasible enough to use with option trades. Many times options might lose twenty-five to thirty percent of their value before, then, *turning around and gaining* an additional ten or twenty percent in profit for the trade.

Not to mention the fact of the initial percentage losses we, as options traders, must face even before we begin to trade, just from the price of the *spread* alone.

Therefore, it is best to either increase your stop losses to forty or fifty percent, or not to use a stop loss at all on quick trades. I understand that this goes against most conventional trading wisdom, which teaches us that we should *always* use a stop loss, but there are times when we need to use mental stop losses along with our eyes, to truly, know when it is right to exit a trade.

Furthermore, a few trading gurus have reported that most of the big smart money managers do not even use a stop losses. Instead, they suggest that stop losses allow the big money investors to, (sometimes) move the markets in such a way as to forcefully swing it back and forth enough to hit the stop losses set by the little retail traders, before then resuming its initial trading direction to profit from the move.

This does happen, but let us be **very clear**; big money is *not always responsible* for choppy, turbulent markets. Oftentimes, it has to do with the news about the U.S. economy or news of some global economic crisis somewhere on around the world.

Many times the markets shift so quickly that even the smart money investors *lose very large amounts money*. Yet, it is still better to be safe than sorry, so, if nothing else, use a ***trailing stop***, which trails only the profitable trades up and only stops us out once a trade starts losing a certain percentage of value, thus allowing us to lock-in, at least some of our profits.

How to Use the News

We must be **very cautious** when making trades based solely on the Financial News. Most trading experts will tell us not to use *any* of the information given from financial news sources, for making trades. Yet, for the most part, they are *correct*. The financial news outlets usually *lag* most large movements of the major markets, because they must take the time to check out sources in order to remain accurate and reliable.

The results of this is that they usually only release the news after most of the major wall street traders and investors (the smart money) have already been privy to the news. Therefore, markets will have already begun to move in the direction of the latest breaking news, before the public even becomes aware of it.

Yet, the financial news media is *still very important* to market trading. Without them, most traders, including many of those who profess to have *never* used the financial news, would find themselves trading blindly, and would ultimately end up losing all the money in their trading accounts. There is a happy medium here, however, where we can both disregard some news stories (that do not really pertain to us), but properly utilize other important news releases to our advantage.

First, we must understand that we encounter multiple sources of financial news media on a daily basis. There exists the business news channels, or news segments on cable television, that exclusively focus on corporate and economic news.

Next, we have the oldest original sources of financial news, the actual printed business newspapers, and magazines, which are widely read around the world. Third, we have radio news segments; and finally the internet financial news media, that has an ever-increasing broad range of news coverage, and is gaining widespread popularity.

Market traders from all backgrounds, at times, can find themselves literally *inundated* with financial news information 24 hours a day.

The correct question is how we can distinguish between the necessary news releases and the more trivial news stories.

The answer lies in the sources behind each of the news stories. What news can actually change the markets' direction? It is simple, when we follow the financial markets over a period of months and years; we begin to discover at least two major sources that move the markets almost like none other.

These sources are the U.S. government's periodic economic reports (such as the monthly non-farm job reports, the GDP, etc.), and the Federal Reserve interest rates announcements and forecasts. Then, adding to those two main sources, you have the price of oil and other global economic upheavals that affect all markets around the world.

Sudden wars and unforeseen attacks breaking out, in unlikely places, most often have a significant affect the global marketplace, as well. Nevertheless, no other factors seem to have a greater effect on the general market climate than when the FED, for instance, announces a new interest rate hike or the monthly non-farm jobs reports, or unemployment reports released by the Federal government.

It is from these two sources of breaking news releases and reports that we should *seriously* consider the news as we are contemplating our trading strategy.

CHAPTER SIX

Working the Trading Plan

Now that we have learned the different elements of our trading strategies and methods, it is time to weave them into a practical plan of action. It is time for us to start putting our trading plan to work in real time. Since we have just sacrificed the time learning to earn extra income by trading options, it is now time for some action.

For a demonstration of all that we have learned, we want to introduce a fictitious trader, who we will call: *trader Jan*. Trader Jan will demonstrate for us, many of the methods that we have just learned for trading options during a normal trading day.

Trader Jan is a person who has saved and accumulated a trading account of about forty-three hundred dollars. She understands that, although this is a lot of money to her and to most people, it is a very small investment to the large smart money investors in the trading world. Therefore, she does not intend to jump right into any trades without first developing a good trading strategy and correctly learning to trade options to earn extra income.

Jan has done her research on the multiple option strategies, which she can use, and on other strategies for trading stocks. Now she feels that she is ready to trade in the NDX options market, as if it was her online business.

GETTING STARTED

Before she commits any real money to trading, however, she wisely decides to trade with virtual money (for paper trading), while still treating those virtual funds as if they were *real* money.

Jan has already picked a reputable online broker that has a good virtual trading platform. Furthermore, she has made sure that she has set aside the *time* necessary to trade during normal U.S. stock market trading hours.

Next, Jan has chosen to start her trading as a Day trader, giving her some valuable experience in this area. She understands the risks of day trading, but prefers to stay in the market in as little time as possible while she is trading.

Next, in order to test every typical market condition that she will encounter, in a real time trading scenario, she decides to load her virtual funds above the twenty-five thousand dollar mark. Thereby giving her the opportunity to day trade five days a week (which covers the normal trading week) instead of just three days (for accounts with less than twenty-five thousand).

Jan further realizes that, although her virtual account has tens of thousands of dollars in it, she will only use less than four thousand dollars per trade, in order to gain real time experience with the amount that she can really *only* afford to trade.

Later, she will limit her virtual trading account to only forty-three hundred dollars in total, similar to her real account, to enable her to test to see if she *finally* has learned the trading skills necessary for successfully trading with real money.

Jan starts her trading day by first referencing the date and noting, in her journal, any *relevant* pre-market conditions that she sees in the market news. She takes note of any developments, which may affect that day's market climate. Trader Jan will be sure to note, in her journal, the calendar day, month, and year, mainly for keeping a good record, which she can refer to later.

Jan will follow the Dow, the NASDAQ, and any important economic news before she decides to commit to any trades. She will be looking for the following things before she enters any trade:

1. First, consistent directional momentum (through volatility) in the Dow and NASDAQ that follows any sudden jumps or leaps in price value, regardless of the direction it is in.

2. Next, news of any weekly or monthly economic reports from the U.S. Federal government, or from other influential government bodies located across the globe. In addition, she scans for any comment, speeches, or congressional hearing testimony released from among those in the FED (Federal Reserve) leadership (such as the FED chair, or district Presidents) regarding interest rate hikes.

3. Third, she will watch out for any candlestick chart set-ups where long wicked candlesticks (on the high side or the low side) signal a reference point where candlesticks will breakout, as long as there is a confirmed move beyond that point. Alternatively, have reverse in the opposite direction if the wick (or tail) points in the direction of the trend.

4. Forth, she will note when the price is above the 20 EMA, 50 SMA, and 8 EMA for Call options or below the 20 EMA, 50 SMA, and 8 EMA for Put option positions. She, also, realize that this strategy is somewhat subjective and should not be the main determiner of her overall strategy.

5. Finally, she will be looking for contradictions in the sum total of price movement, indicators, candlestick chart set-ups, and economic news.

She knows that unless most of these trading elements agree, the market can become too choppy and dangerous for her to enter.

Trader Jan's Plan to Enter & Exit

When trader Jan sees market momentum going in a certain direction that is in line with other market conditions that she notices she will go to her options chain section and buy an NDX option. She just wants to buy an option that represents the direction of the current market trend. If the market becomes too choppy before she enters, however, Jan will stay out of the market, and only enter once the market has chosen a particular directional pathway.

Now Jan will notate, in her trading journal, each trade that she enters into including the price change of the NDX, the Delta she uses, and the value of the Dow when she entered the trade. She will try to keep good notes that she can use later.

Jan will conservatively choose a strike price at or around the thirty point Delta. Moreover, she will only buy an option that has at least anywhere from two weeks to six weeks to expiration (depending on her risk level). She realizes that she will have to pay more for an option that is farther away from its expiration date, but she is ok with that. Jan clicks on the trade button, which, then, allows her to inspect her trade before she actually clicks to buy into the trade.

She must take the time to make sure the trade that she is about to enter into has the correct expiration date, strike price and the amount that she is willing to pay. In addition, before Jan will click-on the final buy button, she decides to go back and *check* on the market conditions, one last time, just to ensure that the market is on the *same trajectory*, as it was previously on when she decided to enter the trade.

Trader Jan has learned to view each trade from the mindset of a businessperson. Therefore, she will limit her risk as much as possible by setting-up a stop loss on the trade to automatically exit the trade once it loses fifty percent in value, or she might *only* add a trailing stop to lock-in her profits, before the market turns against her. Because she will only want to exit the position once the NDX has moved more than ten to twenty *dollars* a share in price change, she will become profitable even before her stop triggers.

At times, this will be extremely difficult for Jan to do; after all, she might be getting out too early. However, from a business standpoint, she realizes that she cannot become greedy by trying to grab every single dollar of the potential profit on each trade. If she is greedy and waits too long to exit, the market will often suddenly change directions, without warning, and turn her big profits into great losses.

Maybe, thirty to forty percent of the time with this exit strategy, Jan will painfully miss some potentially large profits. Yet, about sixty to seventy percent of the time, trader Jan will find that had she stayed in that position for too long, the market would have severely lost its momentum or changed direction altogether, and she would be faced with a losing trade. Hence, during those times when she misses out on large profits because she has exited a position too soon, Jan will remind herself that the smaller profits which she did earn, was the money that she was *safely supposed* earn for *her* set level of risk.

Trader Jan also, will remember that only those willing to gamble with a higher risk level; will be able to receive those profits. In the end however, the shifting markets will eventually cause them to lose all of their gains with such dangerous risks.

There will be days when Jan will not even need use a stop loss if she discovers that there is great volatility in the market, which is moving in the same sustained direction of her position. In addition, if she, also, knows that she will not have to stay in the market for too long.

On the other hand, Jan might put on a *trailing stop* to secure her profits and allow the profits to ride before exiting the trade. On the other days when she uses a stop loss, and the market swings heavily in the opposite direction of her trade with multiple surges, she will not wait until her stop loss is hit, instead she will exit the market *quickly* so that she can cut her losses short.

Then, Jan encounters those trading days when the market is just choppy, and is swinging from one direction to the other. Her strategy for those days is monitor the market throughout the trading day, but if she does not see the market move in a definite, sustained direction, with the necessary momentum to back it up, she will not be trading that day.

She firmly realizes that if she does enter a trade on those days when she has not yet seen the market start to move in one sustained direction, for the most part, she will have to exit the trade early with a loss, or face having her stop-loss triggered with a much bigger loss. At some point, Jan will have to learn to become comfortable staying out of the market altogether.

Jan will, none-the-less, be sure to note in her trading journal, every fifteen to twenty minutes, the price change of the NDX, the change in the Dow, and the current value of her option when she is in the market. She will do this to keep a good record of the market movements during each of her trades both for her personal learning and for future reference.

Once she sees that the NDX has gained an additional ten to twenty dollars in price change, and the market is beginning to pull too far back, she will mark it down in her journal and probably exit the trade without even waiting for her trailing stop. By doing so, she will become consistently profitable with each of her trades.

In time trader, Jan becomes more proficient in her trading. Although it will take a while, Jan will soon discover that she is consistently earning extra income. Eventually, if she stays disciplined in her trading, she will earn enough to pay off her bills, put money away for retirement, and begin trading full time. In the end, trader Jan will come to realize that she has ***uncovered a jewel*** of a trading technique that is unlike any that are out there on the market today.

THE END

PLEASE LEAVE A REVIEW

THANK-YOU

NOTES:

www.ingramcontent.com/pod-product-compliance
Lightning Source LLC
Chambersburg PA
CBHW070958180526
45168CB00003B/1195